© 2014 Juliana Hutchings

© Little Egypt Press

ISBN 978-0692284926

Cover design by Heather UpChurch

Page layout and design by Juliana Hutchings

All rights reserved. No part of this book may be reproduced or transmitted in any form or by any means, electronic or mechanical, including photocopying or recording, without permission from the publisher in writing.

Printed in the United States

Little Egypt Press
145 Winding Trail Loop
Ridge Spring, SC 29129

www.LittleEgyptPress.com

When you read the title of this story: Venture Horse of Dreams, what do you imagine? Surely you think of a special horse that touches hearts and changes lives. But this isn't the story of any person's dream. This is about a mustang horse named Venture, who loved to dream.

To understand Venture's story I must first tell you about his owner. Marty Chubbs was a wealthy but humble man. He lived in Nevada and owned all the land one could see from his farm house.

   Although poor in neighbors, Marty was rich in visitors. People came from all over to visit the ranch. Some thought they wanted to claim his money. But others knew better; They wanted to become his friend.

   You see, Marty owned many horses, and not just the old stock ponies you see in western films, but mustangs as well. Oh yes, mustangs.

Every year Marty and a few of his friends would set out on a wild trek in search of Marty's herd. They would lasso the year-old colts and fillies, and take them back to the ranch for training.

Marty taught them to be all types of horses. The next spring, they were sold, and not long after, their pictures would be in the local papers. There wasn't a foal of Marty's who hadn't grown to be known all over the west.

So as you now understand, people wanted to befriend Marty to help in the grand round-up. The people looked forward to it all year long....and so did some horses.

Blizzard

Blizzard was the strapping stallion of Marty's herd. He had a masculine build, but his worn grey coat suggested his life hadn't been easy. Legend had it, Blizzard was the only horse Marty could never tame. It started long ago when Marty was just a young man, and Blizzard a mere colt.

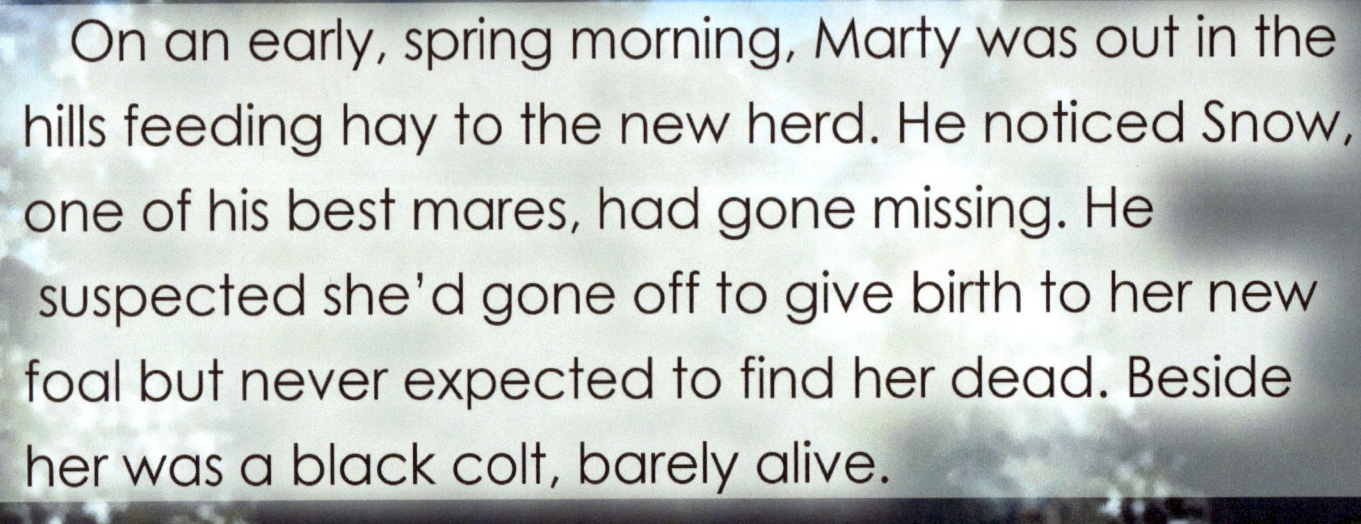

On an early, spring morning, Marty was out in the hills feeding hay to the new herd. He noticed Snow, one of his best mares, had gone missing. He suspected she'd gone off to give birth to her new foal but never expected to find her dead. Beside her was a black colt, barely alive.

From the beginning, Blizzard was a tough creature. Any foal had to be in order to survive without his mother.

Marty took the colt back to his house and nursed him back to health. The next day he turned him over to a ranch mare.

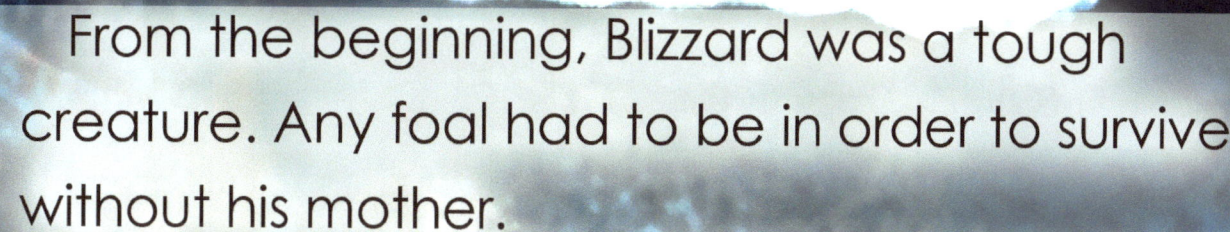

The mare welcomed Blizzard into her family, but the colt refused her offer.

By sunset, Blizzard was gone. Marty saw the broken rail in the corral and sighed. He saddled his trusty trail pony, and went in search of him. Marty found the colt next to his mother's body, nudging her helplessly. When Marty tried to catch him, the colt took off as fast as his spindly legs would take him. He would return to Snow and again, when Marty came near, take off.

They repeated this far into the night. Marty said a prayer for the colt, and feared he would starve, freeze or be attacked by wolves. But it was almost midnight and the freezing air chilled Marty.

He reluctantly left the colt, and went home.

Now of course Blizzard didn't die—I gave that away already. As Marty had suspected, the wolves smelled Snow, but somehow the colt managed to escape.

The next spring at Marty's first roundup, he saw a graying yearling. It was strong and muscled, but scars lined its body. There was no doubt the colt was Blizzard.

Marty wanted him back, but as you may have guessed, he could never catch him.

Eclipse

Born in the same year as Blizzard, was a filly called Eclipse. Unlike Blizzard, she was born in captivity on a dude ranch. The owner was Jake Carlo, who earned the nickname, Jake the Snake.

Snake rented his horses for people to ride. When they returned to the ranch some refused to pay. The lack of money led him to neglect his horses.

One day, a man just as irritable as Snake came by the ranch. He took one of the horses riding for two whole days. This horse was different from the rest. She was due to have a foal any day.

When the man returned, the horse was near exhaustion. He refused to pay for his ride and Snake grew livid. Two hours after the fight broke loose, the police handcuffed Snake and took him to jail. No one was around to help with the birth of the foal.

After two long weeks, the sheriff called Marty Chubbs. The horses needed a new home. Marty wasn't about to turn down horses in need, after all, he was their only chance.

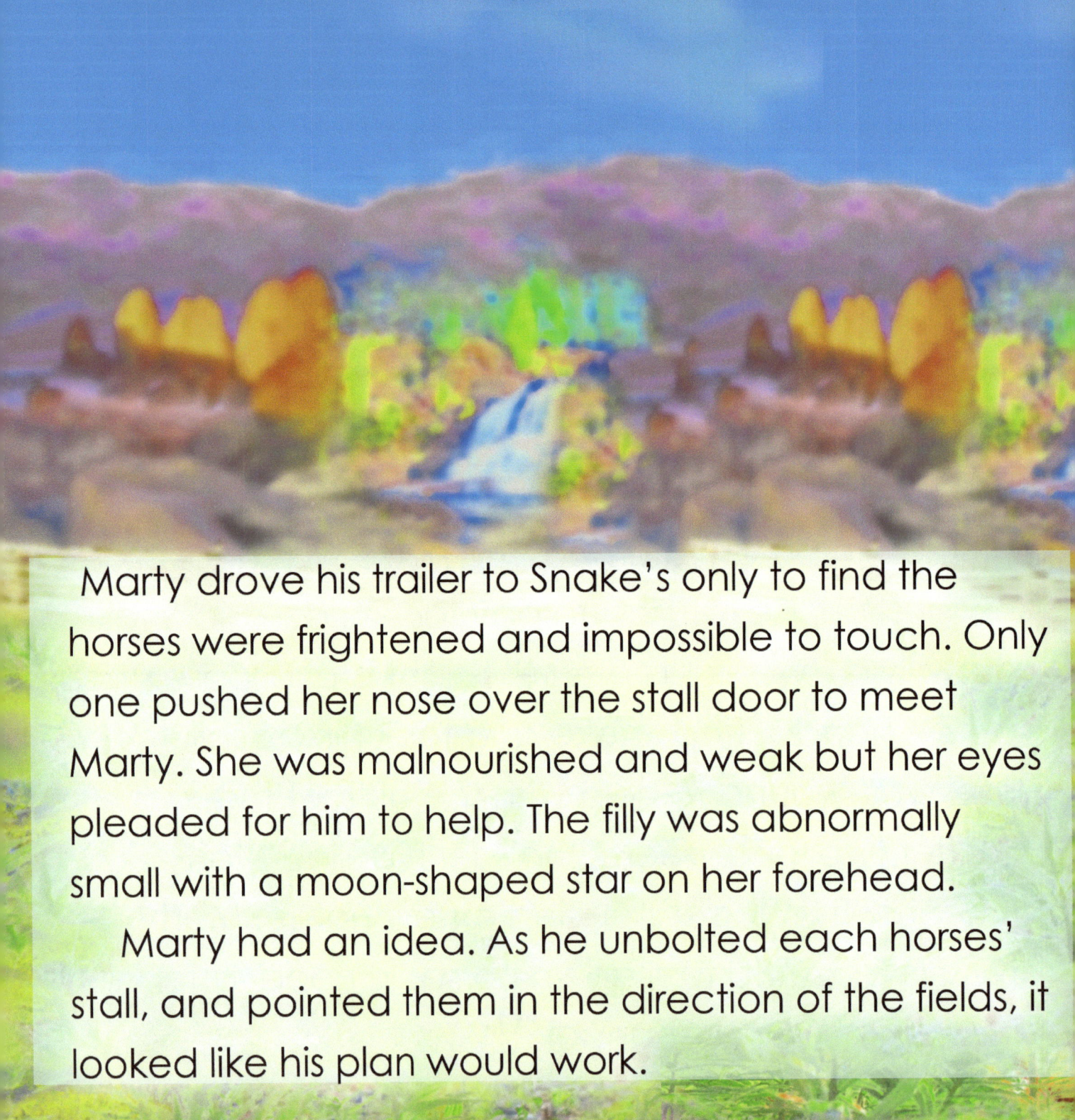

Marty drove his trailer to Snake's only to find the horses were frightened and impossible to touch. Only one pushed her nose over the stall door to meet Marty. She was malnourished and weak but her eyes pleaded for him to help. The filly was abnormally small with a moon-shaped star on her forehead.

Marty had an idea. As he unbolted each horses' stall, and pointed them in the direction of the fields, it looked like his plan would work.

He smiled as the foal galloped alongside her mother, up and over the hills. He would forever call the little filly Eclipse.

Snake's horses found the herd and settled into their new home. Strange as it sounds, they seemed thankful that Marty had given them this wonderful new life.

And so, Eclipse grew, wild and free like Blizzard. She was fast as the wind and had the nose of a bloodhound. For those reasons alone, she became the lead mare of the Nevada herd.

Now that you know all about Blizzard and Eclipse, it's time I tell you about their baby, Venture. He was born in the early spring along with Blizzard's other foals. Named for his adventurous traits, Venture liked getting into mischief. From chasing butterflies, to splashing in the River, Venture enjoyed straying from his mother. For this reason, Eclipse had grown to be protective. She wished her foal would be like the rest, and lie about in the sun all day. She was worried her baby would get lost.

One day, Venture did not come home. It was nearing dusk, and he was nowhere in sight. Eclipse left the dozing herd in search of him. Finally, her nose caught his scent. She tracked the smell and came to a steep cliff. Frantic, she searched the land below.

Marty's ranch lay nestled below the rocks. Corrals lined the earth, and rusty gates trapped horses inside. Eclipse worried what would become of her son.

Suddenly, the rocks began to shift. Eclipse watched as they tumbled down the incline. Fearing wolves had caused the slide, she spun around. Why, it was only Venture!

Venture was reluctant to go home, but he knew it was wrong to wander. He only wanted a better look at the ranch. Just that day, he'd seen last year's colts and fillies in training.

Venture dreamed of how Marty would train him. Would he jump large fences and compete in horse shows? Or would he compete in horse races all over the country? Whatever became of him, Venture was sure it would be a swell life.

Each season brought a new Venture. By winter, he was dreaming of pulling a sleigh through the frosty hills.

When the grass and shrubs became plentiful, and the mustang's wintry coats shed into sleek and shiny hides, Venture practiced routines in the field.

Spring welcomed the new foals, and with it the yearlings were shunned by their mothers. They formed small bands on the outskirts of the herd. Venture, as you may have guessed, was not part of these yearling bands. Too busy dreaming, Venture spent his days watching the training of Marty's horses.

   One morning when Venture awoke, he saw commotion down below. Marty and his friends were saddling the stock horses.

Venture understood—the round up was near!

As the Nevada sun reached its highest point, Blizzard let out a wail so strident it may have been heard from the mushroom farms in Pennsylvania. The horses started at a gallop. The yearlings fused into the main herd, and the foals struggled to keep up with their mothers.

Growing in speed, Marty and his friends appeared over the ridge. They quickly reached the slackers at the back of the herd. One of these slackers was Venture. Now as I have mentioned, Venture was very fast. But as you know, he had big plans for himself.

One by one, the other yearlings were captured. Venture was still free. He pretended to be in complete exhaustion. He slowed to a lazy lope and even put his nose on the ground, begging for air.

"Better toughen up little guy! We've got big plans for you!" called one of the men, just behind Venture. Then he surged past the little mustang, and lassoed the last yearling. Within minutes, the men and yearlings disappeared. The herd went back to grazing and Venture was left heartbroken, confused, and alone.

No one noticed when Venture rejoined the herd. He found his mother, who looked relieved he hadn't been captured. But Eclipse went back to her newest foal. Venture looked to Blizzard for his final hint. The stallion pinned his ears and stamped at the ground in a sign of warning.

It was time for Venture to live on his own. As the months crawled on, he stayed as far from the herd as possible. He spent his days overseeing the training of his old yearling friends.

Venture did a lot of thinking. Marty would want him the following year, Venture was sure. Maybe he was waiting for Venture to grow more. Whatever the reason, he was sure he'd be captured next spring.

And so, spring and summer passed and winter blew in. Venture missed the warmth of his mother and the company of friends more than ever. He longed for the hay Marty tossed to the herd. The icy snow covered what little vegetation was left, and Venture felt his body grow thin.

Just when he thought of giving up, spring arrived. With it came new foals, and the new yearlings formed a bachelor band. Seeing an opportunity for friends, Venture finally decided to join them.

As a two-year-old, Venture easily overpowered the yearlings. He won every mock battle with ease, and soon became their leader. But just like the last year, Marty's annual round-up swallowed Venture's friends.

He was once again left behind.

Venture decided to take action. He had to prove his worth. Surely then Marty would want him as a riding horse.

Venture challenged himself to tests of bravery, speed, and power.

He galloped the steepest hill on the range; He outraced the quickest of wolves, and he jumped the longest of brooks. Before long, nothing fazed him. The once scrawny colt transformed into a horse, strong and mighty.

   As the years passed, only one obstacle remained unconquered. Venture found this challenge truly frightening.

   On the morning of his sixth birthday, he knew he had to face his fear. If he did, Marty would finally see him as a champion.

When night fell, Venture decided to challenge his father. For years, he hadn't gone near the aggressive stallion. But Venture knew age had weakened Blizzard, and the time for battle had arisen.

Suddenly fearless, Venture called to Blizzard in the light of the moon. It was as though the longtime leader knew his son awaited him. He emerged from the shadows and the fight began.

For an old stallion, Blizzard held brutal strength. Venture returned every bite and kick with twice the strength. He wasn't giving up, and Blizzard sensed it. For hours, they fought, squealing, striking, stamping their hooves.

Father and son battled until the dawn sun rose over the mountains. Blizzard began to waver, and finally fatigued. Dropping to his knees, he bowed his head and lay down to rest.

At that moment, Venture realized his future did not lay in a ranch or show ring. He had challenged his father, and he had won. That meant one thing: the herd belonged to Venture. It was suddenly clear what Marty had planned for him all along. Venture was destined to watch over the other horses and lead the Nevada herd.

And that's what he did. Venture ruled the Nevada herd for many years.

Each year the herd grew and grew and with it so did the number of champion yearlings Marty trained for the West. Venture was proud to call them his own, but even more so, he was proud of his freedom.

Marty called his stallion Mighty Venture. He made special trips to visit him and even treated him to carrots and apples.

As the years went by, Mighty Venture never wished to be anyone else. He loved his life. He realized he always had been, no matter how his dreams had mislead him, a mustang...

And a leader at that.

Meet the real life *Venture*

Hutchings wrote *Venture, Horse of Dreams*, when she was thirteen-years-old. "I wanted to write and illustrate my own story," she says, laughing now because she didn't turn out to be an artist. Eleven years later, Hutchings hired an illustrator to help her finish her dream of publishing her first children's book. What inspired her to finish a work created so long ago? The birth of "Mighty Venture" in 2013, whom Hutchings named after her fictional character.

MightyVenture pictured with Juli

"My mom bred our mare, Verbena, to a talented German stallion, named Mighty Magic. The name just magically worked my story." Hutchings put the two names together and her real life inspiration lay before her eyes. She hired an illustrator and sent off photos of the real colt to bring the story to life.

"I have big dreams for this little guy," says Hutchings, who shakes her head and corrects herself—"this BIG guy; he's going to be a very special horse."

Meet the *Illustrator*

The artist, K. G. Krousie is shy and artistic, almost recluse. She loves family, nature, and kindness, finding beauty nestled in the hills and valleys she calls home. She lives among the rivers and bluffs near the Great Mississippi River. She can be found most days engulfed in her art, or seeking a beautiful scene or unique moment in time, to capture on camera or in her art.

Visit Venture on facebook!
www.facebook.com/VentureDreams

Don't miss other titles by Juliana Hutchings

Ages 9-16

Visit us on facebook!

www.facebook.com/ahorsetorememberseries

www.ingramcontent.com/pod-product-compliance
Lightning Source LLC
Chambersburg PA
CBHW042124040426
42450CB00002B/56